LIFE in the Future

ROBOTICS

Mark Beyer

HIGH
interest
books

Children's Press®
A Division of Scholastic Inc.
New York / Toronto / London / Auckland / Sydney
Mexico City / New Delhi / Hong Kong
Danbury, Connecticut

Book Design: Christopher Logan
Contributing Editor: Jennifer Silate

Photo Credits: Cover, 37 © Sam Ogden/Science Photo Library/Photo
Researchers, Inc.; p. 4 © Corbis; p. 7 © Hank Morgan/Photo Researchers,
Inc.; p. 8 © Roger Ressmeyer/Corbis; pp. 11, 18, 29, 31, 34 © AP/Wide World
Photos; p. 12 © Timothy A. Clary/AFP/Corbis; pp. 14, 17 © James
King-Holmes/Science Photo Library/Photo Researchers, Inc.; p. 21 © Klaus
Guldbrandsen/Science Photo Library/Photo Researchers, Inc.; p. 22 © Julian
Baum/Science Photo Library/Photo Researchers, Inc.; p. 25 © Peter Menzel
Photography; p. 26 © Bettmann/Corbis; p. 32 © Reuters NewMedia
Inc./Corbis; p. 38 © N. Nicolaou; p. 41 © Darren Winter/Corbis

Library of Congress Cataloging-in-Publication Data

Beyer, Mark (Mark T.)
Robotics / by Mark Beyer.
     p. cm. — (Life in the future)
Summary: Takes a look at the current state and future of the field of
robotics, emphasizing that robots are already playing an important role
in making our lives easier.
Includes bibliographical references (p.) and index.
ISBN 0-516-23918-X (library binding) — ISBN 0-516-24007-2 (pbk.)
1. Robotics—Juvenile literature. [1. Robotics.] I. Title. II.
Series.

TJ211.2 .B49 2002
629.8'92—dc21

                                        2002002074

CONTENTS

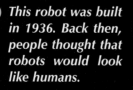

This robot was built in 1936. Back then, people thought that robots would look like humans.

The word *robot* comes from the word *roboto* in the Czechoslovakian language. It means doing a job over and over. The playwright Karel Capek first used the term in 1923 to describe human-like machines. In his play, *R.U.R.*, robots do the work of people. The robots go out of control and kill the humans. Since then, people have wondered about the future of robotics and what it will mean for humans. Will our super-smart robot creations take over the world? Will humans become their servants?

What do you think of when you hear the word *robot*? Do you think of the fictional humanlike machines that appear in the movies? It may surprise you that most real robots don't look anything like humans. It may also surprise you that robots are already at work all over the world. Robots are no longer the stuff of science fiction. Robots work in factories, with the military, and in hospitals. There may even be a robot in your home already! Scientists are working to create robots that feel, see, and think all on their own. Every year, robots get smarter and smarter. Some scientists believe that a robot that's as smart as a human will be created by the year 2050. Let's take a closer look at the future of robotics—and how it will affect almost every part of our lives.

TECH TALK

A robot called the SlugBot is being made in England. It can catch more than 100 slugs in an hour. Scientists are trying to figure out how to use the slugs to make electricity.

The HelpMate transports medicine, food, and supplies in hospitals.

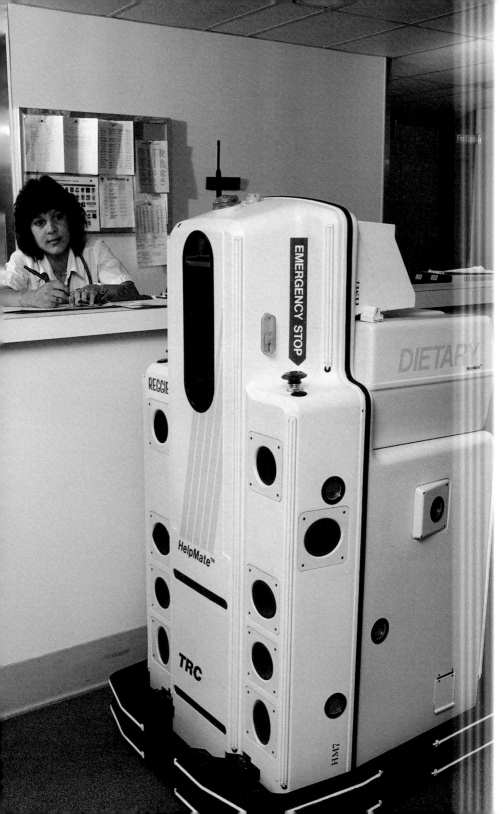

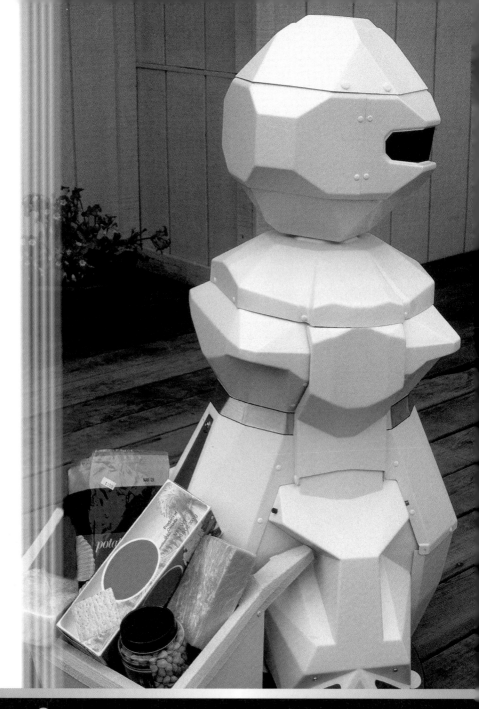

Personal robots, like this one, may soon be in homes around the world. This robot brings food to its owners.

CHAPTER ONE

Robotic Nation

Robotics is the science of making machines that do the jobs of humans. The jobs that robots will do range from the most common, like cleaning, to the most important, like saving lives.

The last thing anyone wants to do after a day's work is household chores. Today, robot lawn mowers are already trimming the grass at some homes. Not too far in the future, robotic vacuum cleaners will be ready to enter our homes, too. As technology gets more and more advanced, robots will do more things for us. Some day, we may not ever have to work again.

DANGER SEEKERS

Robots will be used to do dangerous jobs for people, too. Policemen, firemen, and soldiers risk their lives every day. If robots can do the most dangerous work for them, many lives could be saved.

Hagen Schempf of the Carnegie Mellon University Robotics Institute in Pittsburgh, Pennsylvania, has built two robots that may soon be used to do dangerous jobs. The Omniclops is a 6-inch (15 centimeters) sphere with a camera inside. The Omniclops can quickly reveal what is in, on, or around a dangerous area. It can be thrown through a window into a house or building. The Omniclops can also be dropped into a sewer or down a well for search-and-rescue operations. It will allow the authorities to get the facts they need—without risking anyone's life.

When the Omniclops isn't the answer, a miniature robotic vehicle can be. Schempf has also built the Mini-Dora, a remote-controlled, four-tracked vehicle that can climb stairs. With its own onboard camera, the Mini-Dora can peer into rooms and hallways. Shigeo Hirose of the Tokyo

This robot is being used to check a suitcase that is thought to have a bomb inside.

Institute of Technology also makes robots to save lives. His robot, the Blue Dragon, can look beneath the rubble after an earthquake or other disaster. Like the Mini-Dora, the Blue Dragon is also remote controlled.

Many earthquakes or other disasters leave small holes and tunnels that can stretch for hundreds of feet under the rubble. In order to rescue survivors of disasters, police and rescue teams must know where to look. However, most of these areas are only a few inches wide. Hirose's Blue Dragon and Schempf's Mini-Dora can move through these tunnels because they're small.

Both the Blue Dragon and the Mini-Dora are made to climb over rough, uneven surfaces. These mini robots can easily scale jagged rocks and broken brick or glass. Best of all, if they tip over, they can pick themselves up and keep on going. Their cameras send back images of what is in the rubble to rescue teams. The robots are equipped with listening devices, too. The devices can pick up sounds of trapped people's movement or breathing. Right now, these robots are still being tested in laboratories.

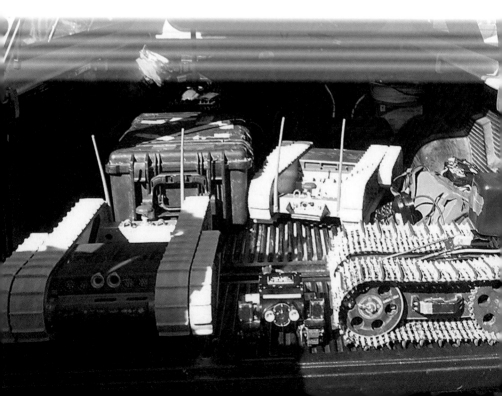

TECH TALK

After an earthquake in Mexico City, 135 people died while trying to rescue others. About 40 different rescue robots are being researched right now so that more people won't be injured or killed while trying to save others.

Search-and-rescue robots have already been used to look for survivors buried under rubble. One robot that has seen action in the field is called Urbie. It can flatten itself to the size of a pizza box to fit through small holes. Urbie can also lift itself up to crawl over things. It has video sensors that act like eyes to help it get around obstacles. Urbie also has voice-activated microphones that can be used by rescue teams to hear people who are trapped. Like the Mini-Dora and the Blue Dragon, Urbie can also be thrown into places where people cannot go. Urbie is even being used by the military to scope out possibly dangerous areas.

These robots are used to search through rubble after disasters.

Dr. Peter Kyberd developed this myoelectric hand. It can hold objects and do more, much like a human hand.

CHAPTER TWO

Our Bodies, Our Bots

Handling household chores and helping police, military, and rescue teams is only a fraction of what the future holds for robotics. Robotics is also being used to help the human body do its job. Scientists are working on many new and amazing ways for robotic machines to help our bodies.

MORE THAN HUMAN

Robotics has helped people who have lost limbs to be more independent and productive than ever before. The days of using a wooden stump or a plastic hand in place of missing limbs are over. Those devices didn't provide the users with a way to move the replaced limbs. Today, mechanical legs, arms, knees, and hips are very common. Prostheses, or replacement limbs, now have computer chips, electronic sensors, and motorized wheels, wires, and joints. These robotic limbs allow people to walk, bend down, and pick up objects without help from others.

Myoelectrics is the latest technology used in prosthetics. Electrical signals in your body make it possible to move your muscles. The electrical signals from muscle movements in the body of a person who has lost a limb move the prosthesis. These electric signals are a million times weaker than the electricity needed to power a light bulb. Electronic sensors in the prosthesis pick up the signals and move the limb. The sensors are able to read body temperature, direction of movement, and position of the limb.

Getting a myoelectric limb to work properly is not easy. The right muscles have to be moved to make the limb move correctly. This takes a lot of practice for the user.

Right now, myoelectric prosthetic hands move only the thumb and the middle and index

New prosthetic hands will be covered with artificial skin. They will be able to do almost everything that a human hand can.

fingers. These three fingers can be moved together to hold objects, such as tools and silverware. In the future, prosthetic hands that can move each finger will be available. These kinds of robotic hands already exist, but they're too expensive for everyday use. Before they are available for the public, they will be used by National Aeronautics and Space Administration (NASA) astronauts in outer space.

Right now, the C-Leg is only worn by about 300 people, but it's thought that many more people will be using it soon.

Breakthroughs are also being made in creating robotic legs. Engineers are working to find better ways for people to move, walk, and run. They are working with much of the same technology that's used for prosthetic hands. However, legs must help us keep our balance and support the weight of our bodies. This means that a prosthetic leg must be much stronger than a prosthetic hand. But it cannot be so heavy that the user can't lift or move it.

Scientists have been working with microchips and sensors to make a "smarter" prosthetic leg. They hope to make a leg that will be able to adjust its movements while the person wearing it is walking. Using motors and hydraulic joints, the leg will be able to adjust for uphill and downhill walking without a problem. Right now, there is only one leg that uses robotic technology that is available for use. It's called the C-Leg. The knee in the C-Leg can adjust itself fifty times every second. However, the C-Leg is very expensive—it costs $40,000! But as time goes on, this technology will become more afford- able. Prosthetic legs of the future will have robotic knees, ankles, feet, and leg sockets. In time, scientists hope that people with disabilities will never have to use wheelchairs.

SURGERY-BOTS

Robotics is also being used to help doctors do their jobs. Scientists have developed robotic tools that can be used in surgery. These surgical tools are thinner than a human finger. They have devices at their ends that can cut or clamp skin, tissues, or body organs. Each tool can move in six different directions.

The surgeon sits behind a console, or control panel, during the operation on the patient. Working in front of a video screen, the surgeon moves the instruments using a kind of joystick. A small camera on the robotic tool allows the sur- geon to see what he or she is doing.

Surgeons have successfully used robotic arms to perform brain surgery.

Successful surgeries using these tools have already been done in German hospitals. Their robotic surgical system is called the da Vinci Surgical System. Many surgeons believe the da Vinci system will soon be used in the United States.

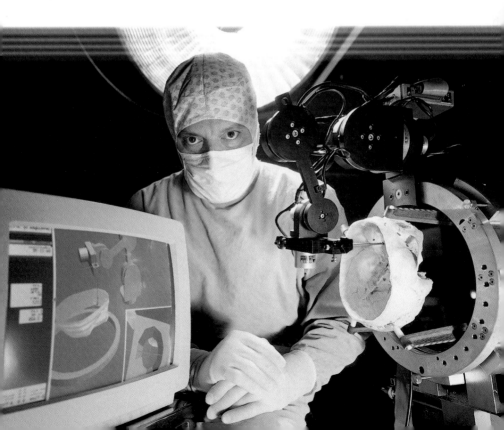

INNER SPACE

Nanotechnology is the science of building things that are as small as atoms or molecules. Not too far into the future, nanotechnology may be the key to curing deadly diseases. Engineers are working on processes in which thousands of tiny robots may be injected into our bodies. These robots can be designed to fight cancer cells and other causes of illness. If the technology works,

TECH TALK

The first person to use robotic technology was Leonardo da Vinci. More than 500 years ago, da Vinci made a device that was supposed to move like a bird's wings.

robots like these can be used to alert our doctors to illnesses even before any symptoms show.

Nanotechnology may seem like something out of a science-fiction novel, but it's not. Right now, researchers around the world are successfully making smaller and smaller robots.

SMART DUST

Professor Kristopher Pister is an electrical engineer working on miniature robots at the University of California at Berkley. Pister likes to think small—*very* small.

Pister calls his robots Smart Dust. These tiny machines will have sensors that can read temperature, their location, and the direction they

As shown in this illustration, future robots may be small enough to be injected into a person's body to fight illnesses.

are moving in. They'll even be able to move from place to place. Many robots can already do these things, but Pister's robots will be different. Each particle of Smart Dust will only be 1/8 of an inch long!

If Pister is successful, the uses of Smart Dust are endless. Children could carry Smart Dust robots in their hair or on their clothes. If a child is missing, the robots could tell the child's location in minutes. Likewise, doctors and nurses could use these robots to watch elderly patients. If a patient falls or has a seizure, the hospital staff could be alerted immediately. At home, Smart Dust with special sensors could be sprinkled on food to tell if it's spoiled.

Today, Pister's miniature robots can only measure the temperature in a room. But Pister and his students are working on ways to make the Smart Dust even smarter. In time, they hope to see their dreams of Smart Dust come true.

Millions of Smart Dust robots could one day fill the air, performing many different tasks.

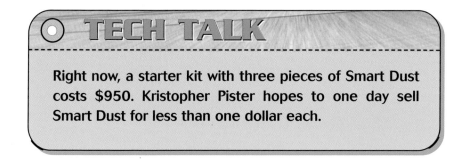

⊙ TECH TALK

Right now, a starter kit with three pieces of Smart Dust costs $950. Kristopher Pister hopes to one day sell Smart Dust for less than one dollar each.

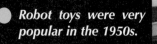

*Robot toys were very
popular in the 1950s.*

CHAPTER THREE

Robo Toys

Robotics isn't just all work. The first robot toy was made in the 1930s. It was made of tin and could only move its arms. Since then, toy technology has gotten much more advanced. Today's robot toys come in many shapes and sizes. Toys can now walk, talk—and even learn!

MY REAL ROBOT

In November 2000, the Hasbro toy company and the iRobot robotics company began to sell their newest doll, My Real Baby™. This doll is not like any other doll ever made. My Real Baby™ has incredibly lifelike rubber skin. It was made to act like a newborn human baby. It chews when given its "food." It sucks when offered a bottle. My Real Baby™ even laughs when it's tickled.

My Real Baby™ uses computer and electronic technology to make it move and react to human touch. Motors move its arms, legs, and body. Gears beneath the skin move metal parts that make facial expressions.

The realism of My Real Baby™ takes off when it begins to talk. Like a real baby, the My Real Baby™ doll must learn to talk. At first, it only coos. Eventually, it learns to say things like "I love you, Mommy," and "Night, night."

THE NO-MESS PET

For kids and families who cannot own an animal, there is now the battery-powered robotic dog, AIBO®.

AIBO®'s owners must train their robot dog. AIBO® can learn to play with a ball, lie on its stomach, and move its paws. Using computer technology and a camera, it can even recognize people when they come close. When AIBO® is ignored, it will find its ball and begin playing

AIBO® can play with a ball and even other AIBO® toys.

alone. It kicks the ball around and chases it. When its batteries are low, the mechanical dog lies down and goes to "sleep."

Aibo means "pal" in the Japanese language. More than 100,000 AIBO® robots have been purchased around the world. Right now, AIBO® costs around $900.

TOYS OF TOMORROW

Toys are becoming more and more advanced with each passing year. The movie *Toy Story* showed a world where toys talked and worked with one another. This may not be fiction for long. Someday soon, robotic toys will be able to have conversations with us and each other. Who knows what the toy boxes of tomorrow may hold?

FUN AND GAMES
RoboCup

Soccer is a sport played by people all over the world. Now, even robots are getting in on the action! RoboCup is an international soccer league conference for robots and their creators. RoboCup is like soccer's World Cup games, except robots, not human athletes, are scoring goals. It takes researchers up to a year to design, program, and build their robots. Kids can enter the RoboCup Junior competitions.

Robot engineers from around the world gathered to watch the final small robot match in RoboCup 2001.

Each year, robot engineers bring robots of all sizes to the RoboCup soccer matches. There are different leagues for the various sizes and types of robots: small (robots that are the size of soft-balls), middle (robots that are the size of small children), and Sony AIBO® robots.

There is also a computer simulation league that is a kind of soccer video game in which the computer plays itself; no actual robotic players are used. The simulators are considered robotic because they use a form of artificial intelligence to play the games.

The robots competing in the RoboCup games must make every move and play on their own. They are not remote controlled. Sometimes the robots are clumsy, falling over or scoring against themselves. But each year, the robots get better.

In the 2001 RoboCup, 111 teams from twenty-three different countries attended. This RoboCup had the first rescue-robot event. In this event, robots (like the Omniclops or the Blue Dragon), which are used to help rescuers find victims, competed in different situations. In the 2002 RoboCup, a humanoid, or human-shaped robot, league will be started. It will be the first time that humanoids will play soccer.

The ultimate goal of the RoboCup conference is to have robots that are smart enough, and skilled enough, to beat the human World Cup champions by the year 2050. The research that is done in preparation of the games is used to help with real-life problems. One day, teams of robots may even be used to build structures on Mars!

AIBO® dogs don't always make a goal, but with help from their programmers they are getting better.

The Asimo robot looks like and can move like a human. It can adjust its step on its own—even when walking down stairs.

CHAPTER FOUR

Robots Among Us

Robots have appeared in movies since the 1920s. Robotic technology has been used to make dinosaurs, aliens, and even ghosts come to life. Filmmakers use robotics to create realistic-looking effects. In movies, we only need to believe that what's happening on the screen is real. But in real life, robots have to work.

A COSTLY RECEPTIONIST

The Honda automobile company in Japan has been working to build a humanoid for years. In 1996, it unveiled the P3. The P3 was able to walk down stairs and open doors. The P3 was one of the first humanoids that successfully moved like a person.

In 2000, Honda introduced a new robot, Asimo. Asimo is 4 feet tall and weighs 114 pounds. It can turn, and change its step, without stopping. The P3 was programmed to walk but could only move as it was programmed. Asimo can adjust its step while walking on its own. Honda's robots keep getting more and more advanced. In 2001, a new Asimo was released. This Asimo is more flexible than the 2000 version and can speak! The new Asimo can say about one hundred different things. Honda plans on renting out their robots for about $166,000 a year. One company plans on using an Asimo robot as its receptionist!

A COG IN THE MACHINERY

Researchers at the Massachusetts Institute of Technology (MIT) are also working on robots that behave like humans. Right now, they are hard at work trying to create a robot with artificial intelligence. Artificial intelligence is a goal that many

Cog has special cameras that it uses as eyes to "see."

robot researchers and scientists want to achieve. These scientists and researchers don't want the robot to understand algebra, they just want it to think like a human being. MIT researcher Rodney Brooks is working on a robot called Cog. He hopes that Cog will be as intelligent as a six-month-old baby. This may sound easy, but it isn't. He wants the robot to think on its own, just as a baby would.

Right now, Cog can watch what someone is doing and imitate that person's actions. Cog has only a torso, arms, and a head, but it's the most advanced robot around!

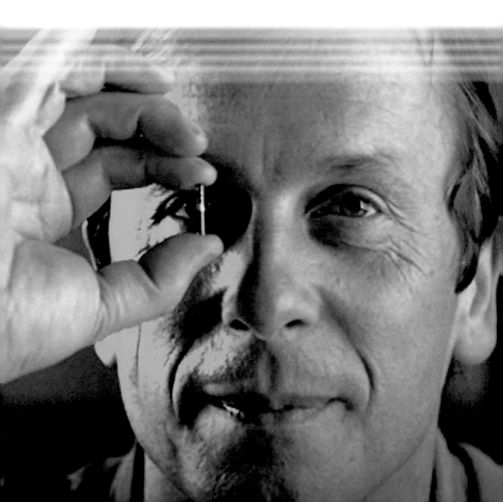

MR. ROBOTO

While some scientists are working to build a robot with human qualities, others are working to give humans robotic qualities. Professor Kevin Warwick, a scientist in England, is doing just that. He wants to be superhuman with robotic parts; he wants to be a cyborg. He believes that people will eventually evolve into cyborgs. This may sound like science fiction to most of us, but not to Professor Warwick.

In 1998, Warwick put a computer chip into his arm. The chip communicated with computers in his lab and told them where in the lab he was. The computers opened the doors in the room for him when he went near them. In 2002, Warwick put a chip into his arm that is connected to his nervous system. He hopes to one day put a similar chip into his wife's arm. Warwick hopes that he and his wife will be able to share their feelings through the chips.

Kevin Warwick holds up the small computer chip that he had implanted into his arm, in 1998.

These are the first steps toward meshing man with machine. With this technology, people one day may be able to get extra memory implanted into their brains. Imagine being able to remember everything you ever saw or read! This technology may also be used to implant identification chips into our bodies. A computer would be able to tell where we are at every moment. But in the wrong hands, this could be bad news. As technology becomes more advanced, we have to be careful that it is used wisely.

LOOKING AHEAD

What exactly is the future of robotics? We know we are moving toward a world where robots play an important role. Advancements in robotics for medicine, health, entertainment, law enforcement, and everyday chores are being made daily. But will we live in a world where robots look like humans, think like humans, or talk like humans? If this happens, will it be a bad thing? And what

● *Someday in the future, cyborgs may no longer be science fiction.*

would happen if robots become as smart as humans? Should they be treated like humans? Will robots have to follow the same laws that people do? Will they have the same rights as people? Right now, these questions are hard to answer. But there's no doubt that the world of tomorrow will be an exciting and challenging one for us all.

artificial intelligence the ability of a machine to imitate intelligent human behavior

computer simulation an imitation of a real situation created on a computer

cyborg a human that has robotic parts

humanoid a robot that resembles a human

hydraulic operated or moved with the pressure from water that is moved from a large space to a smaller space

microchips very small pieces of machinery

myoelectrics a technology used in prosthetics that uses the electrical signals from a person's muscles to move a robotic limb

nanotechnology the science of building things that are as small as atoms or molecules

prosthetics the medical branch that involves designing, making, and fitting replacement limbs

robotics the science of making machines that do the jobs of humans

sensors electronic parts that are able to read things like temperature, direction, and position

Smart Dust tiny robots that are created by Kristopher Pister and are 1/8 of an inch long

technology the use of science and engineering to do practical things and to make life longer, better and easier

Gifford, Clive. *How to Build a Robot*. Danbury, CT: Franklin Watts, Inc., 2001.

Iovine, John. *Robots, Androids, and Animatrons, Second Edition*. Blacklick, OH: McGraw-Hill Professional Book Group, 1997.

Jones, Joseph L., Anita M. Flynn, and Bruce A. Seiger. *Mobile Robots*. Natick, MA: A.K. Peters, 1998.

Lunt, Karl. *Build Your Own Robot!* Natick, MA: A.K. Peters, 2000.

Searle, Bobbi. *Robots*. Boston, MA: Advantage Publishers, 2000.

Vogt, Gregory, and Deborah Shearer. *Robotix Robot Inventor's Workshop*. Philadelphia, PA: Running Press, 2000.

Organizations

American Nuclear Society
Robotics and Remote Systems Division
555 North Kensington Avenue
LaGrange Park, IL 60525
(708) 352-6611

American Society of Mechanical Engineers (ASME)
345 E. 47th Street
New York, NY 10017

Association for Unmanned Vehicle Systems (AUVS)
1735 North Lynn Street
Suite 950
Arlington, VA 22209-2022
(703) 524-6646

Web Sites

MIT Humanoid Robotics Group
www.ai.mit.edu/projects/humanoid-robotics-group/
This Web site has information about Cog and other robots that are being developed at MIT.

RoboCup
*www.csl.sony.co.jp/RoboCup/New/html/
  building_robots.html*
This Web site has all of the latest information about upcoming and recent RoboCups.

The Tech Museum of Innovation
*www.thetech.org/exhibits_events/online/
  robots/teaser/*
This site is run by The Tech Museum of Innovation. Learn all about robots and robotics. Find out how robot engineers are building animal robots and listen to interviews of engineers.

INDEX

About the Author

Mark Beyer is a writer and editor whose interests include science, history, biography, and literature. He lives outside of New York City.